Carolyn Miller's

BOOK 1

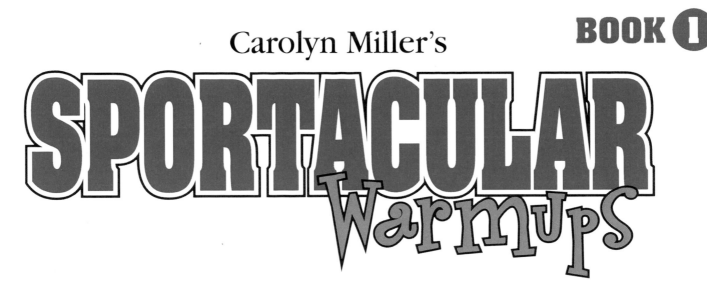
SPORTACULAR Warmups

PREFACE

The purpose of this series is to increase the student's technical ability. Each book contains material designed to strengthen fingers, increase flexibility, and help the student master the many technical skills needed to perform well. *Sportacular Warmups* combines sports and music. Students can relate the musical exercise to a similar activity in the five sport areas. As a review, each section ends with a solo that incorporates various exercises from that section.

I hope students will enjoy *Sportacular Warmups* and will become "sportacular" pianists!

Carolyn Miller

CONTENTS

PLAYBACK+
Speed • Pitch • Balance • Loop

To access audio, visit:
www.halleonard.com/mylibrary

Enter Code
6531-8042-9613-2110

ISBN 978-1-4584-1964-4

WILLIS MUSIC

EXCLUSIVELY DISTRIBUTED BY

HAL•LEONARD®
7777 W. BLUEMOUND RD. P.O. BOX 13819
MILWAUKEE, WISCONSIN 53213

Visit Hal Leonard Online at
www.halleonard.com

ABOUT THE COMPOSER

Carolyn Miller's teaching and composing career spans over 40 prolific years. She graduated with honors from the College Conservatory of Music at the University of Cincinnati with a degree in music education, and later earned a masters degree in elementary education from Xavier University. Carolyn regularly presents workshops throughout the United States and is a frequent adjudicator at festivals and competitions. Although she recently retired from the Ohio public school system, she continues to maintain her own private studio.

Carolyn's music emphasizes essential technical skills, is remarkably fun to play, and appeals to both children and adults. Well-known television personality Regis Philbin performed her pieces "Rolling River" and "Fireflies" in 1992 and 1993 on national television. Carolyn's compositions appear frequently on state contest lists, including the NFMC Festivals Bulletin. She is listed in the *Who's Who in America* and *Who's Who of American Women*.

In her spare time Carolyn directs the Northminster Presbyterian Church Choir in Cincinnati, Ohio and enjoys spending time with her family, especially her seven grandchildren.

I.
BASKETBALL

1. Dribbling

2. "Box Out"

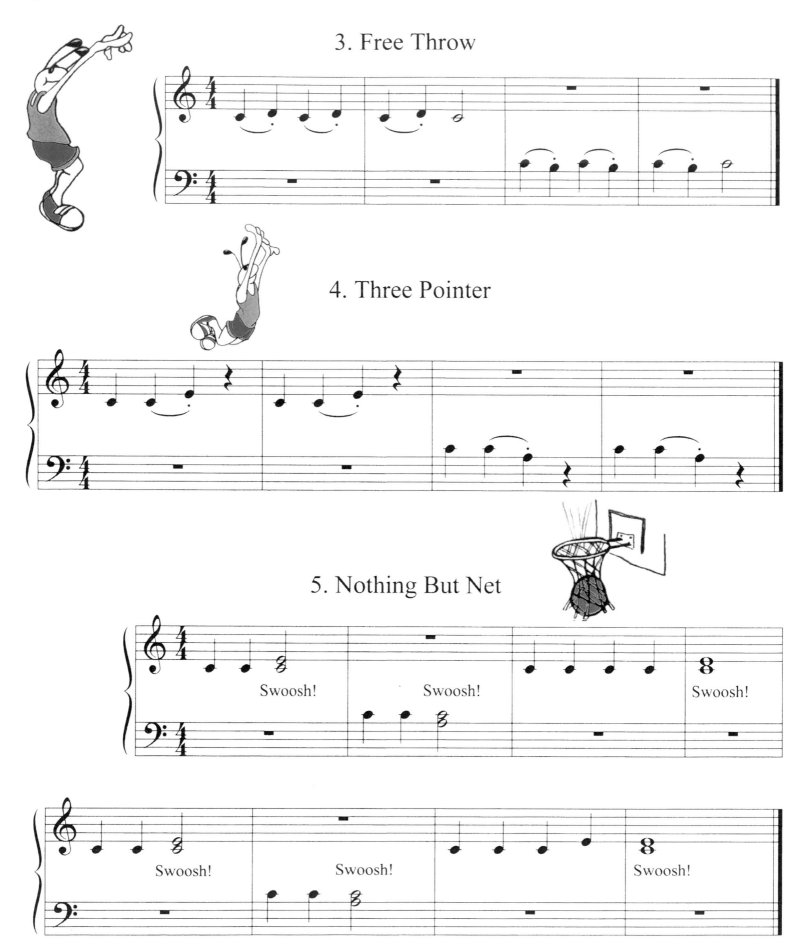

6. Lay Up

7. Jump Shot

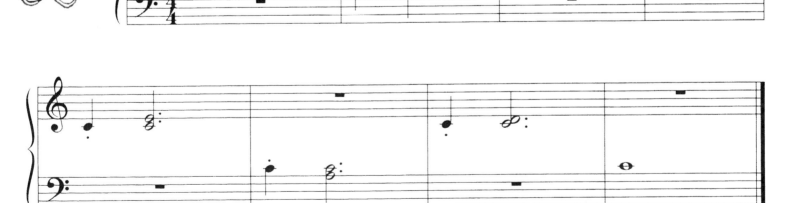

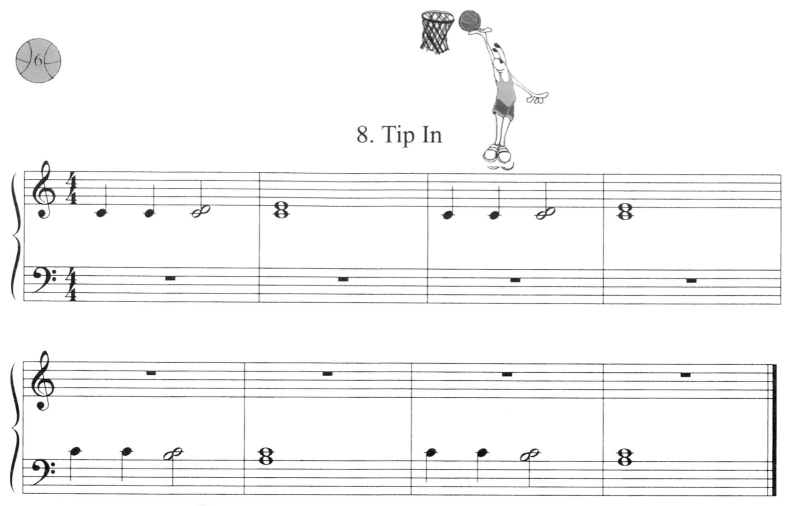

8. Tip In

9. Foul

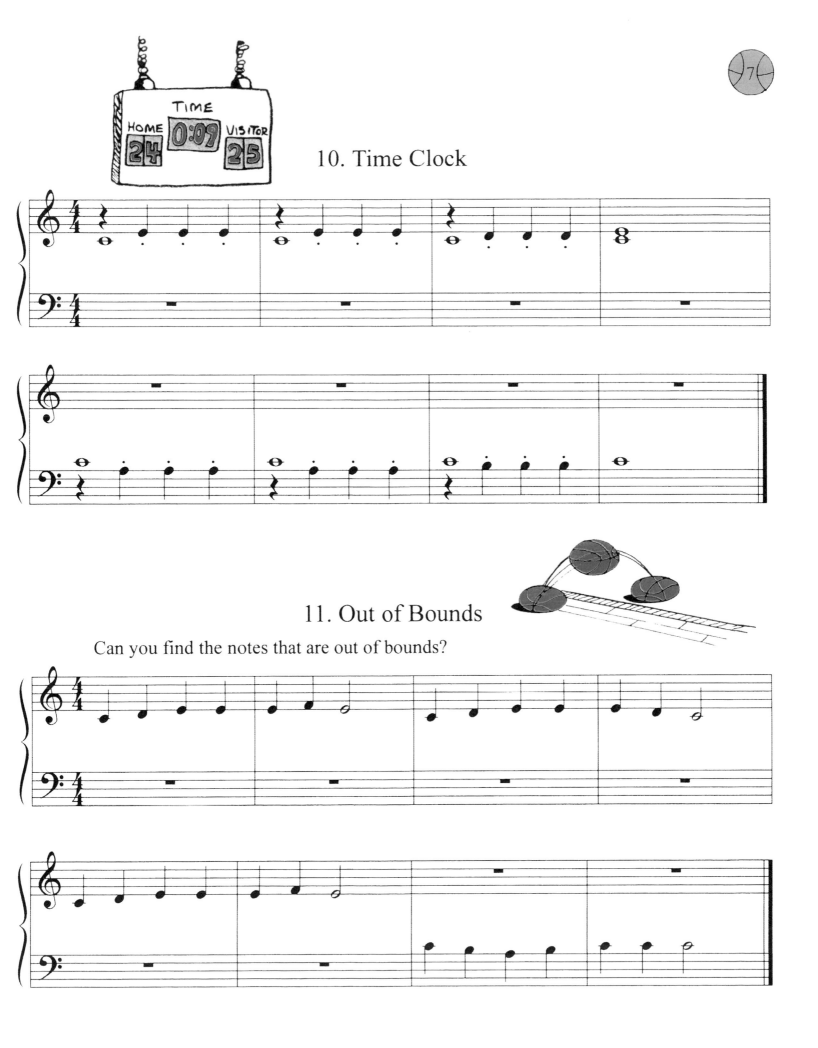

10. Time Clock

11. Out of Bounds

Can you find the notes that are out of bounds?

12. Overtime

II.
BASEBALL

1. Bunt

2. Single

3. Double

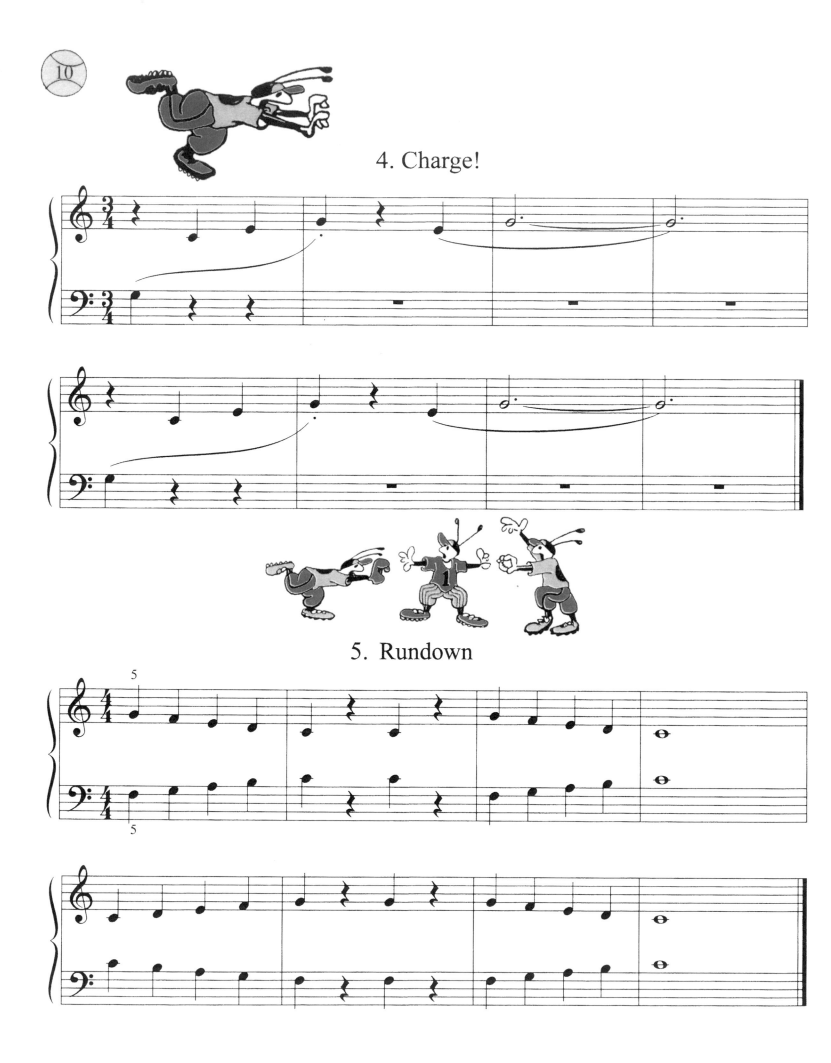

4. Charge!

5. Rundown

6. Seventh Inning Stretch

7. Slow Curve

8. Line Drive

9. Homerun!

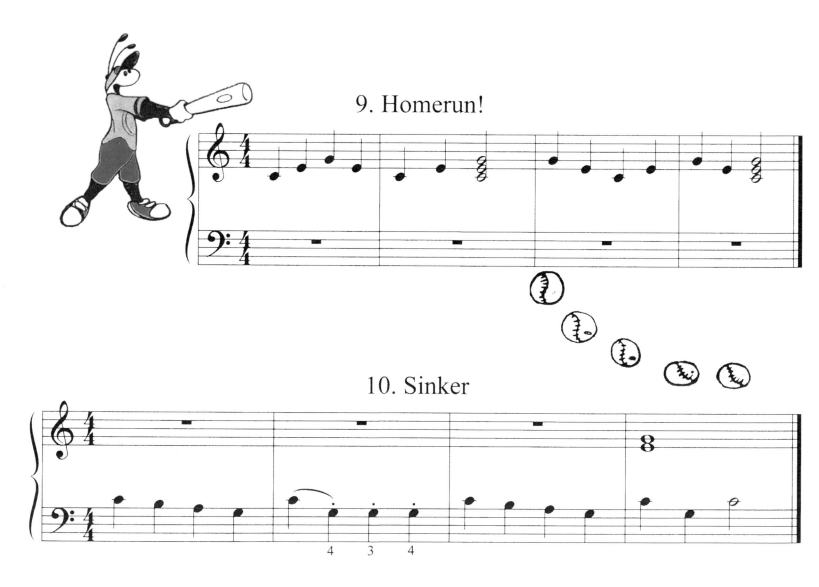

10. Sinker

11. Pop Fly

12. Blooper

Extra Inning

III.
TRACK AND FIELD

1. False Start

2. Hurdles

3. Triple Jump

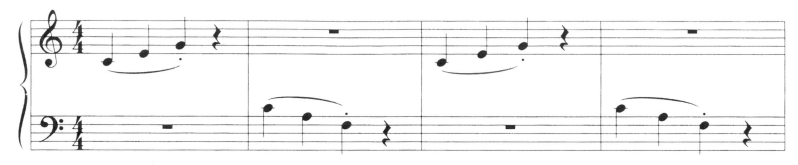

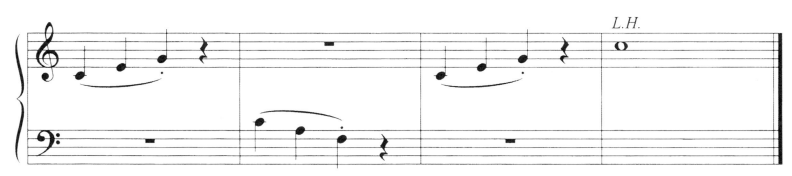

L.H.

4. Go for the Gold

L.H.

5. Pole Vault

6. Long Jump

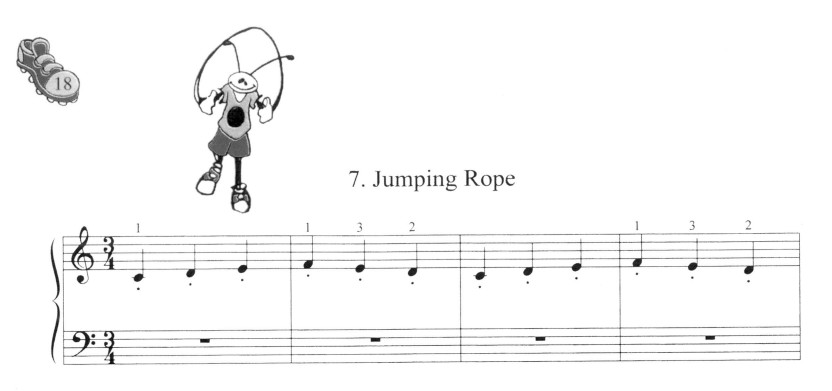

7. Jumping Rope

8. City Finals

IV.
EXTREME ADVENTURE SPORTS

1. Rappelling

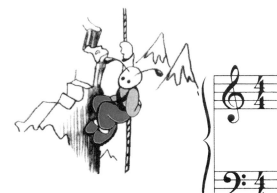

2. Bungee Jumping

3. Skateboarding

4. Nervous Skateboarder

5. Mountain Climbing
(Little Mountain)

6. Big Mountain

7. Wheelie

8. Free Fall

9. Shooting the Rapids

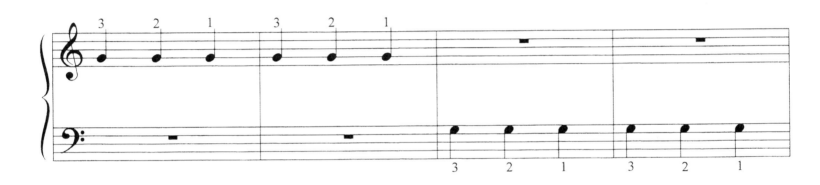

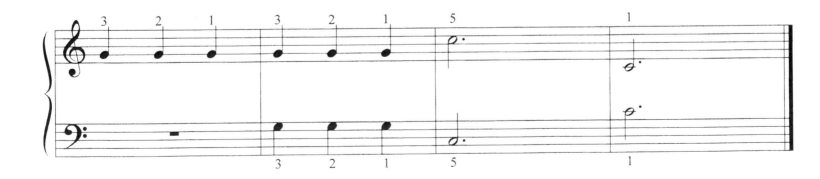

10. Hang Ten

11. Hang Ten to the Limit

12. Take the Risk

V.
SOCCER

1. Passing

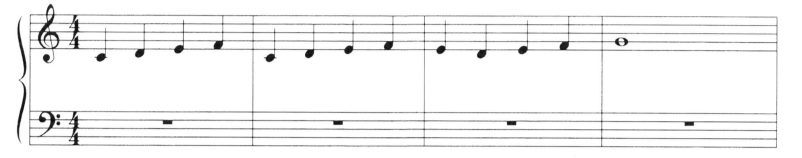

2. Break Away Pass

3. Penalty Kick

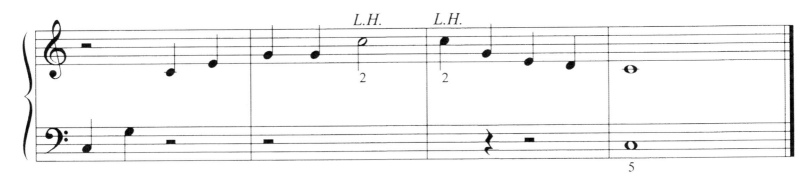

4. Goal Attempt

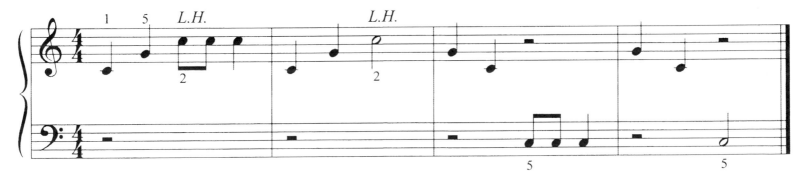

5. Charging

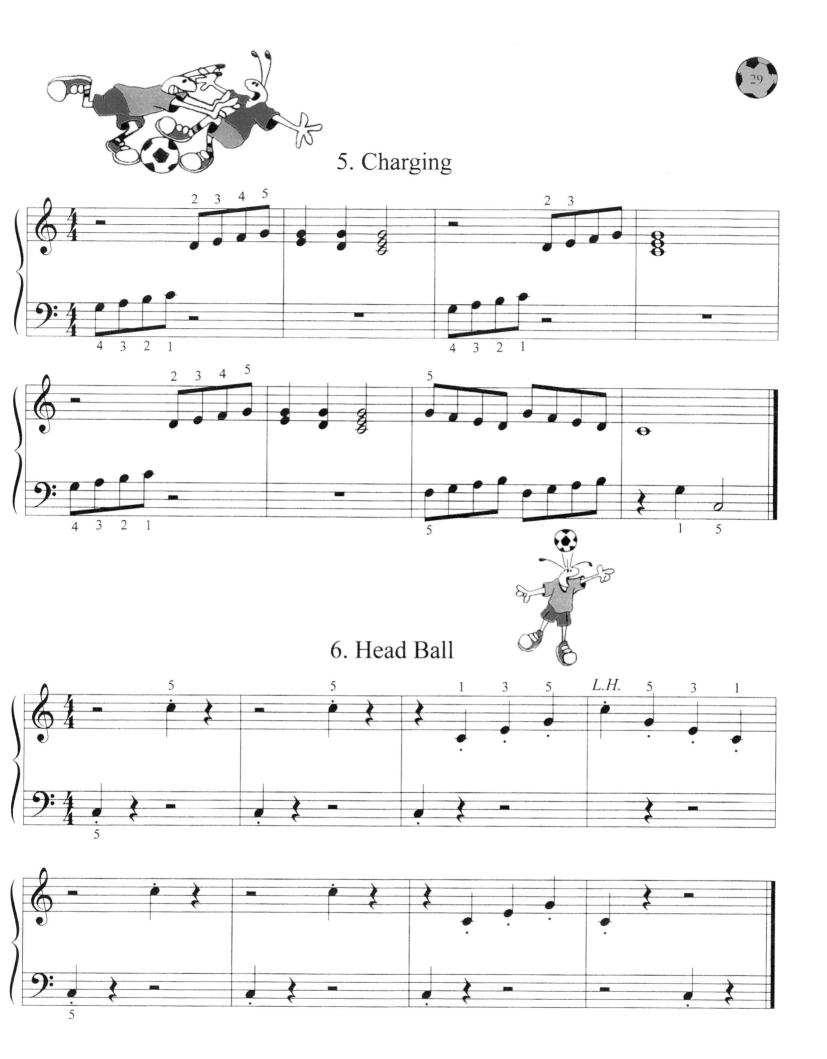

6. Head Ball

7. Body Block

8. Dribbling Up and Down the Field

9. Out of Bounds

Which notes are out of bounds?

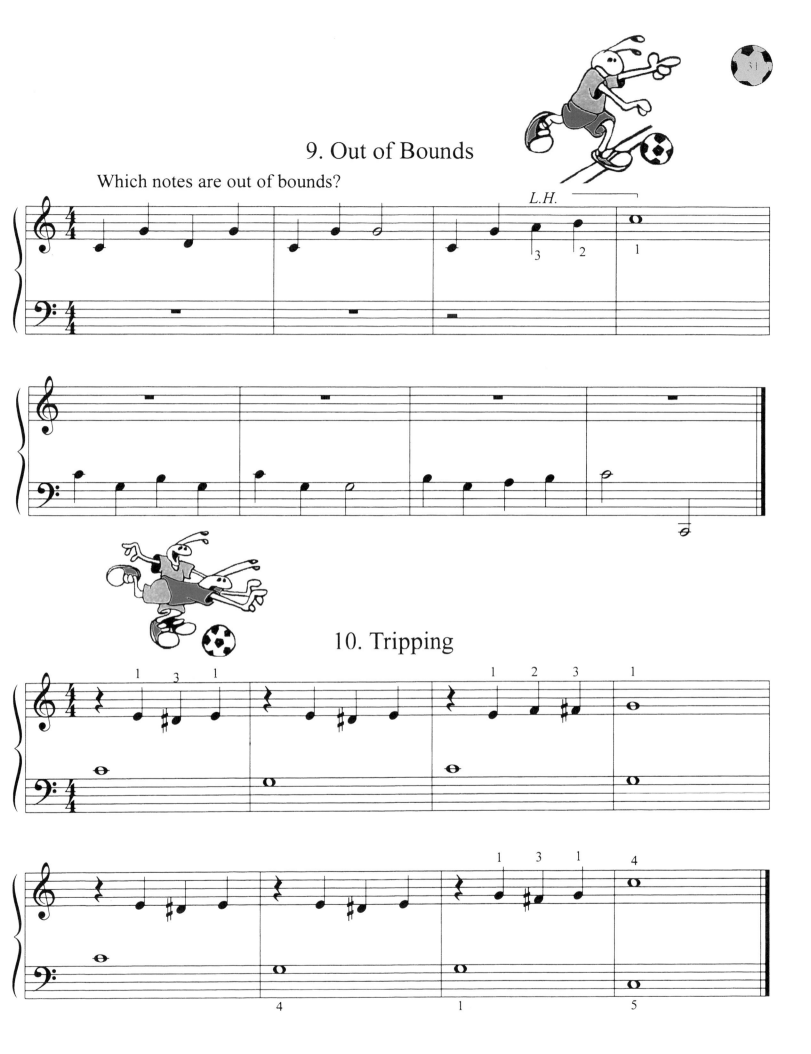

10. Tripping

11. Game Day

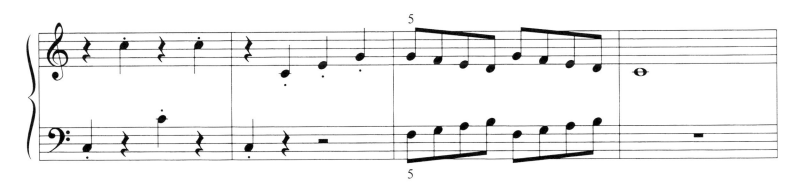

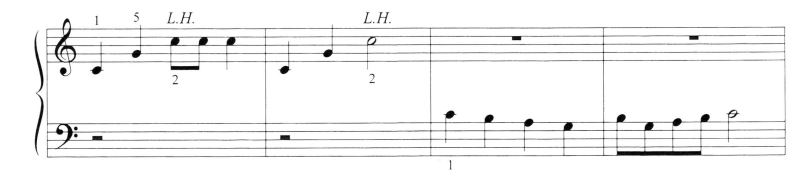

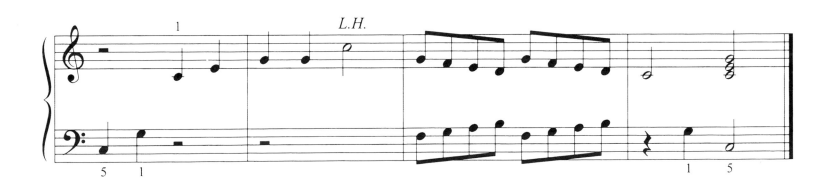